W9-CFB-909

BASEBALL

by Jonatha A. Brown
Reading consultant: Susan Nations, M.Ed., author/literacy coach/consultant

WEEKLY (WR) READER®
EARLY LEARNING LIBRARY

Please visit our web site at: www.earlyliteracy.cc
For a free color catalog describing Weekly Reader® Early Learning Library's list
of high-quality books, call 1-877-445-5824 (USA) or 1-800-387-3178 (Canada).
Weekly Reader® Early Learning Library's fax: (414) 336-0164.

Library of Congress Cataloging-in-Publication Data

Brown, Jonatha A.
    Baseball / Jonatha A. Brown.
      p. cm. — (My favorite sport)
    Includes bibliographical references and index.
    ISBN 0-8368-4337-1 (lib. bdg.)
    ISBN 0-8368-4344-4 (softcover)
    1. Baseball—Juvenile literature.   I. Title.
  GV867.5.B743   2004
  796.357—dc22   2004041988

This edition first published in 2005 by
Weekly Reader® Early Learning Library
330 West Olive Street, Suite 100
Milwaukee, WI 53212 USA

Copyright © 2005 by Weekly Reader® Early Learning Library

Editor: JoAnn Early Macken
Art direction, cover and layout design: Tammy West
Photo research: Diane Laska-Swanke

Photo credits: Cover, title, Gregg Andersen; p. 5 © Hulton Archive/Getty Images; p. 6
© Al Messerschmidt/WireImage.com; p. 7 © Stephen Chernin/Getty Images; p. 9 Tammy West/
© Weekly Reader Early Learning Library, 2005; pp. 10, 18 © Elsa/Getty Images; p. 12 © Tom
Cammett/WireImage.com; p. 13 © Allen Kee/WireImage.com; p. 14 © Doug Pensinger/Getty
Images; p. 15 © Gary Lake/WireImage.com; p. 16 © Tom Hauck/WireImage.com; p. 19 © Jamie
Squire/Getty Images; p. 20 © Jed Jacobsohn/Getty Images; p. 21 © Chris Hardy/WireImage.com

Printed in the United States of America

1 2 3 4 5 6 7 8 9 08 07 06 05 04

Table of Contents

CHAPTER 1

Baseball Then and Now

People have played games with a bat and ball for a long, long time. Some of the old types of games had funny names like "rounders" and "one old cat." These games were played in the 1700s.

As time went on, some of these games began to look more and more like baseball. Soon, baseball clubs were formed. Rules were written. More and more people got hooked on the great sport of baseball.

Young British women play rounders in this photo from 1948.

The umpire, catcher, batter, and pitcher watch the ball closely during a Little League game in Florida.

Today, millions of people love the game. Kids play baseball in school and in Little League. On weekends, they round up their friends and play in backyards and parks. When they grow up, many join baseball clubs. They want to keep playing ball.

Many of the best players play professional baseball. Most young pros start in the minor leagues. Many make it to the major leagues. Each team has its loyal fans. Many fans go to ball parks to watch their favorite teams play. Others watch games on TV.

Fans cheer the team from Harlem, New York, during a Little League World Series game.

CHAPTER 2

Baseball Basics

Baseball is played on a flat field called a diamond. Four spots are marked on the field. These spots are called bases. Each base has a name. They are first base, second base, third base, and home plate. Players play at these and other positions on the playing field.

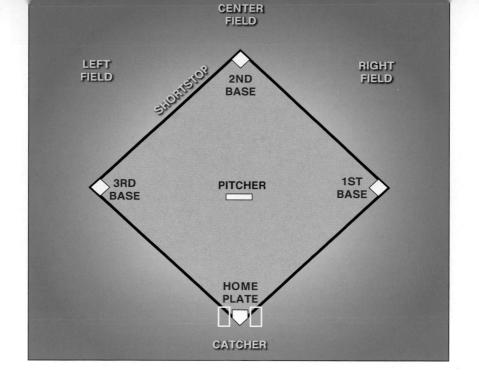

Two teams play against each other. Each team has nine players. The teams take turns trying to hit the ball. This is called being at bat. Players on the team that is at bat try to do three things. They try to hit the baseball, get runners on the bases, and score runs.

A player from the Japanese all-star team slides into home during the Little League World Series. The catcher, from Boynton Beach, Florida, has the ball and is ready to tag the runner out.

Players on the team that is not at bat are in the field. These players try to keep the other team from scoring runs.

The team that scores the most runs by the end of the game is the winner.

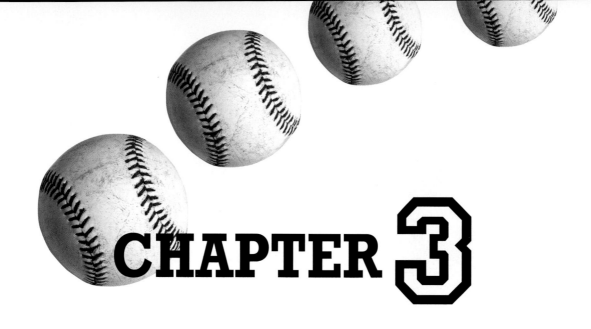

CHAPTER 3

Exciting Moments

Picture this. You are the batter. You crouch over home plate and hold the bat over your shoulder. Your eyes are glued on the pitcher. He stares at you for a moment. He is trying to make you nervous. Then he winds up and throws the ball.

Pitcher Pedro Martinez
of the Boston Red Sox
throws a strike.

The ball flies right over home plate. WHACK! You have swung the bat and slugged that ball! It sails over second base, toward center field. The center fielder runs back, hoping to catch it. But the ball is GONE! It has sailed over the fence and out of the park. You have hit a home run! The crowd rises and cheers as you run around the bases, cross home plate, and score a run. Your teammates greet you at the plate. What a great moment!

Hitting a home run is always exciting. The most exciting home run is called a grand slam. A grand slam can only happen when the bases are loaded. This means that there are runners on all three bases. Then, when the batter hits a home run, all three runners plus the batter score runs. Hitting a grand slam is a quick way to give your team four runs!

Star outfielder Barry Bonds of the San Francisco Giants is unable to rob an opposing batter of a home run. His picture is on the fence!

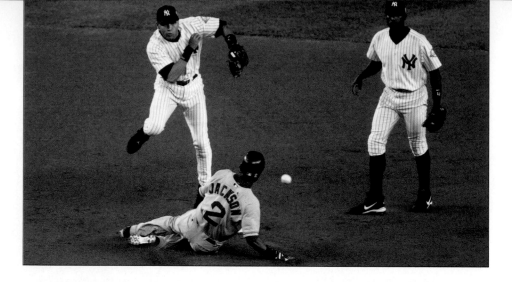

Derek Jeter of the New York Yankees turns a double play against the Red Sox. The runner slides into second base, but he is already out. Jeter's throw will beat the batter to first. Two outs!

The team in the field often makes exciting plays, too. If a ball is hit with runners on base, the team in the field has a chance to get two players out. That is called a double play. Every once in a while, the team in the field gets three players out in one play. That is called a triple play. Triple plays can only happen with at least two runners on base. It takes great teamwork to pull off a triple play.

An infielder fires the ball to throw out the runner in a college game between Kent State and West Virginia.

Baseball is filled with close plays. The bases are loaded with runners on first, second, and third. The batter hits the ball. It is a ground ball. The runners speed toward second, third, and home. A player on the other team scoops up the ball in his glove. He knows he must throw out the runner who is trying to score from third.

Safe at home! The umpire gives the "safe" sign in a game played between the Yankees and the Tampa Bay Devil Rays in Tokyo, Japan.

The ball reaches the catcher just as the runner slides into home. They collide. Did the runner reach home safely? Did the catcher hang onto the ball and tag him out? Is the runner safe, or is he out? It is up to the umpire to decide!

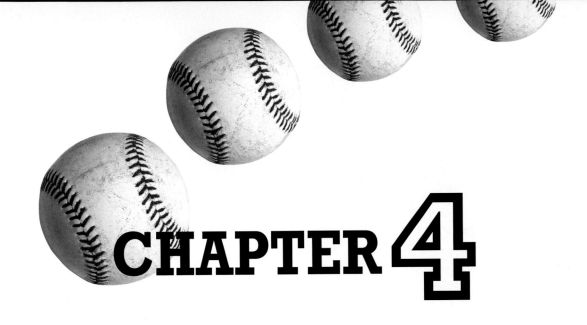

CHAPTER 4

The World Series

Every sport has its champion teams, including baseball. The Little League World Series takes place in Williamsport, Pennsylvania, every August. The best Little League teams from around the world play against each other for ten days. Some games are shown on TV.

One after another, teams lose games and drop out. Finally, only two teams are left. They play against each other. The team that wins is named the Little League World Champion for that year. What a huge thrill for the players and their families and fans!

Players from the Louisville, Kentucky, team celebrate their victory over a team from Japan in the Little League World Series.

A few weeks later, the major leagues hold their playoffs. The winner of the American League playoffs meets the National League winner in the World Series. The World Series is North America's oldest professional championship.

Pitcher Josh Beckett and his Florida Marlins teammates celebrate their victory over the New York Yankees in the 2003 World Series.

The Marlins' Josh Beckett tags out the Yankees' Jorge Posada for the final out in the 2003 World Series.

Fans pay high prices for tickets to World Series games. Millions more watch on TV. The teams play between four and seven games. The first team to win four games wins the World Championship pennant.

When the Series is over, the players and their fans say good-bye for the winter. But soon they are dreaming of Spring Training and the games to come in the next season.

Members of the San Diego Padres work out at their Spring Training Camp in Arizona.

Glossary

crouch – to lower the body by bending the legs

out – removed from play until the next turn to bat

pennant – a flag that stands for a championship. Many pennants taper to a point.

positions – places

professional – playing a game as a paid job

umpire – the person in a sport who rules on plays

For More Information

Books

All-Time Great World Series. Andrew Gutelle (Grosset and Dunlap)

H is For Home Run! A Baseball Alphabet. Brad Herzog (Sleeping Bear Press)

The Illustrated Rules of Baseball. Dennis Healy (Ideals Children's Books)

My Baseball Book. Gail Gibbons (HarperCollins)

Take Me Out to the Ballgame. Jack Norworth (Aladdin)

Web Sites

MLB.com Kids Club
mlb.mlb.com/NASApp/mlb/mlb/kids/index.jsp
Baseball schedules, online games, tips, and news

Science of Baseball
www.exploratorium.edu/baseball/
Use science to improve your game

Index

About the Author

Jonatha A. Brown has been writing children's books since leaving a corporate position in 2001. She holds a B.A. in English from St. Lawrence University in Canton, New York. Jonny lives in Phoenix, Arizona, where she is a fan of the Arizona Diamondbacks. Her favorite sport is dressage.